ANTIGRAVITY PROPULSION

Human or Alien Technologies?

THE UNDERGROUND KNOWLEDGE SERIES

James&Lance
MORCAN

ANTIGRAVITY PROPULSION: Human or Alien Technologies?

Published by:
Sterling Gate Books
78 Pacific View Rd,
Papamoa 3118,
Bay of Plenty,
New Zealand
sterlinggatebooks@gmail.com

Special Note: This title is an extended version of Chapter 29 of *The Orphan Conspiracies: 29 Conspiracy Theories from The Orphan Trilogy* (Sterling Gate Books, 2014) by James Morcan & Lance Morcan. This title therefore contains a combination of new material as well as recycled material (in many cases verbatim excerpts) from *The Orphan Conspiracies*.

National Library of New Zealand publication data:

Morcan, James 1978-
Morcan, Lance 1948-
Title: ANTIGRAVITY PROPULSION: Human or Alien Technologies?
Edition: First ed.
Format: Paperback
Publisher: Sterling Gate Books
ISBN: 978-0-473-36539-4

· · · ● ● ● ● ● ● · · · ·

"Truth will come to light ... at the length, the truth will out."

· · · ● ● ● ● ● ● · · · ·

–William Shakespeare,
The Merchant of Venice, Act II, sc. 2

CONTENTS

• • • ● ● ● ● ● • • •

FOREWORD

· · · · ● ● ● ● ● · · ·

BY GRANT HAYMAN

We can look back on the scientific ideas, or lack thereof, of people long ago and consider how silly and vain people were to think you could fall off the edge of the Earth, to think the Earth was the center of the physical Universe, to think flying machines were impossible or that it was pure fantasy to believe technologies like telescopes could allow you to look into magical other-worlds.

Yet this same arrogance and vanity remains within us even today, for although we admit we are not the center of the Universe, many still loudly proclaim, *We are the only intelligence in the Universe!*

Above: Antigravity tech—a better way to travel?

"Ovni" Licensed under Public Domain via Wikimedia Commons

Is not this idea just a repeat of the same mistake, the same self-importance, of the people in the past?

We like to think our current civilization is the wisest, most intelligent out of all civilizations which have come before and any which may yet exist, but can we be so absolutely certain of this?

Sure, we are masters of the automobile, computer experts and rocket scientists, but is this really the only successful path, the only productive knowledge which can be known by a civilization? Can we be so certain there is no other, easier, better, smarter way or more efficient way to live upon this world and perhaps even to travel amongst the stars to other worlds?

To those interested in traveling to other worlds, especially to other stars, it is painfully clear rocket technology cannot be the way we will bridge these vast distances.

One must consider with all seriousness, if rocket technology does not enable us to master gravity, then the possibility must exist that there is some other technology, some other science which we have yet to discover. A new science which puts these far off worlds within reach and could put our own world, in reach of other civilizations besides our own.

One can argue such conjecture is nonsense and better applied to a work of science fiction.

However, as you will read in this book by James & Lance Morcan, many prominent, highly educated, well regarded and, I might add, completely sane individuals have been quoted affirming "such an advanced new science does exist" and that "there is a new technology which can cause great, positive changes and prosperity upon our planet for all people." Furthermore, and perhaps more importantly, these renowned individuals also claim, "We are not alone in the Universe."

When such influential and respected people make such extraordinary claims, should we so quickly dismiss such ideas?

Do we wish to remain safe at home so we do not fall off the edge of the world, or do we have the courage and humility to seriously consider the precious and valuable glimpse into our own possible future that these pioneering minds are putting before us?

Grant Hayman

Independent advanced propulsion researcher

Founder of OVAL Tech Advanced Interstellar Space Propulsion Systems

INTRODUCTION

· · · ● ● ● ● ● ● ● ● · · ·

In January 2014, it was reported by *The New York Times* and other mainstream media outlets that America's National Security Agency (NSA) uses secret technology to remotely input and alter data on computers worldwide—even when targeted PC's or laptops are not connected to the Internet. This suppressed technology, which uses radio frequencies to spy on computers, only came to the public's attention as a result of leaked NSA documents from former agency contractor-turned whistleblower Edward Snowden.

This begs the question: Is it a regular occurrence for governments, intelligence agencies and the military to withhold scientific breakthroughs from the public?

If so, how many other suppressed inventions exist in the world's ironclad vaults of power?

And what if most of the *futuristic* technologies readers and cinemagoers are presented with in bestselling books and blockbuster movies are not science fiction, but science fact? What if they already exist on the planet, but are suppressed from the masses?

Imagine for a moment a reality where all the technologies that futurists have predicted have already been invented and are currently being used by a privileged few.

There have been numerous reports of scientific inventions that never saw the light of day even though they were perfected and ready to go on the market. Rumors of these radical inventions date back to the post-Industrial Revolution period in the late 1800's and early 1900's, and have persisted right up to and including the present day.

If a documentary film based on the conspiratorial history of suppressed technologies was ever produced, the individuals featured would include everyone from inventors who either suddenly died or went missing or faded into obscurity, to tech investors whose investment plans were mysteriously thwarted, to scientists who lost their patents without receiving any valid explanation.

Above: Futuristic tech props from the movie Total Recall (2012)

San Diego Comic-Con 2011–Total Recall outdoor display (5985865074)
by pop culture geek from Los Angeles, CA, USA
San Diego Comic-Con 2011–Total Recall outdoor display Uploaded by SunOfErat
Licensed under CC BY 2.0 via Wikimedia Commons

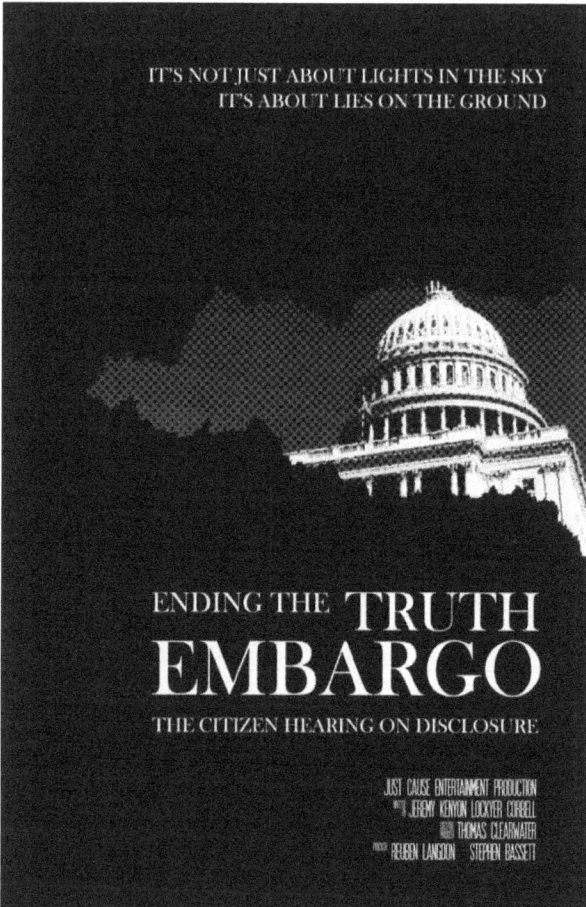

Above: Poster for documentary on UFO disclosure demands

*"CHD Ending The Truth Embargo Movie Poster" by NakedMedia—Own work.
Licensed under CC BY-SA 3.0 via Wikimedia Commons*

And then, of course, there's the Military Industrial Complex with their labyrinth of secrecy—be that in the form of classified science, disinformation or cover-ups.

Our friend and former Japanese Ministry of Defense scientist, Dr. Takaaki Musha, perhaps summarized this subject best when he wrote in the foreword to our book *The Orphan Conspiracies* that he strongly suspects there exists "extraordinary technologies developed by the world's superpowers" and that "most of these technologies have been concealed from the public's eyes."

Later, in that same foreword, Dr. Musha goes on to make this telling statement: "The world's governments have many classified layers and outsiders rarely gain access to their hidden secrets. And certainly no common man can get confirmation of the existence of exotic technologies."

Possibly more than any other exotic science, rumored or otherwise, *antigravity propulsion systems* are the most suppressed—not to mention the most difficult to gather concrete evidence on.

Antigravity propulsion systems are essentially technologies that allow spacecraft to levitate free from the force of gravity instead of traveling in the conventional manner of all other *known* aeronautical and aerospace machines.

Above: A triangular shaped spacecraft
"Blacktriangle."

Licensed under CC BY-SA 3.0 via Wikimedia Commons

This quantum physics-style theory of antigravity spacecraft suggests they are completely free from the force of gravity and this is said to explain the incredible aerial maneuvers of UFO's witnesses have reported seeing all over the world for decades.

These technologies represent what may very well be the greatest scientific mystery of our times.

The key question this book explores in regard to antigravity propulsion is as the subtitle suggests: *Human or alien technologies?*

In other words, are the antigravity spacecraft untold people have reported seeing in our skies actually manmade and the result of long-suppressed, strictly classified inventions by great scientists such as Nikola Tesla and Viktor Schauberger—*or* are they technologies that have been stolen from, or donated or unintentionally left behind by, extraterrestrials?

To do justice to the results of our research, we go off on a few tangents in places—as you'll see. But please bear with us as you read through what we believe to be the main arguments for and against the various theories relating to the mysterious, mind-blowing phenomenon that is antigravity propulsion.

James Morcan & Lance Morcan

1

· · · • • ● ● ● • • · ·

A Covert Civilization

"There exists a shadowy government with its own Air Force, its own Navy, its own fundraising mechanism, and the ability to pursue its own ideas of national interest, free from all checks and balances, and free from the law itself."

–Daniel K. Inouye, US Senator from Hawaii

Assuming working antigravity propulsion technologies do exist, which seems the only logical conclusion given the enormous number of spacecraft sightings reported worldwide, that would likely confirm there is a *Splinter*

Above: Top-secret black triangular craft in an unknown
US Air Force hangar

Civilization that secretly and autonomously resides on our planet right now. In other words, a small, invisible but powerful rogue alliance operating in total isolation from known society.

Such a group's membership would probably be a combination of high-ranking military personnel, senior intelligence agents as well as shadowy government figures and many of the global elite. Although all citizens of various nations and speaking different languages, they would be united by the common goal of attaining mass power, or a New World Order.

Because of its almost infinite sources of funding—mostly derived from black ops appropriations—this Splinter Civilization would have in its possession technologies that would make a layman's mind boggle. The covert civilization would use inconceivable, stealth-like weaponry to wage quiet wars on vulnerable nations. Such weaponry could even facilitate alteration of the weather and the creation of so-called acts of nature.

And of course, *contractors* commissioned by faceless middlemen employed by the shadowy members of this splinter group would, one way or another, silence any investigative reporters or citizen journalists who come close to uncovering evidence of its existence.

Sounds like a theory we should reserve for our other careers as filmmakers and novelists?

You'd be right thinking such theories should be reserved for fiction-based entertainment– except for one important point. Many of these suppressed technologies, including antigravity propulsion systems, have been reported by former engineers and other employees of the Military Industrial Complex. And the list of whistleblowers is an extensive and impressive one that dates back decades.

Researching the reports of those same government insider whistleblowers, combined with the aforementioned (mainly but not exclusively) civilian sightings of UFO's, it is possible to *connect the dots* and at least envisage a hazy picture of what the Splinter Civilization's classified aerospace technologies are.

And one of the most important dots that any serious UFO investigator needs to connect other dots with is: Area 51.

"This thing has gotten so highly-classified … it is just impossible to get anything on it. I have no idea who controls the flow of need-to-know because, frankly, I was told in such an emphatic way that it was none of my business that I've never tried to make it to be my

business since. I have been interested in this subject for a long time and I do know that whatever the Air Force has on the subject is going to remain highly classified"

–Senator Barry Goldwater, Chairman of the Senate intelligence committee

2

AREA 51

"In my opinion I think they were worried that it would panic the public so they started telling lies about it. And then I think they had to tell another lie to cover their first lie, now they don't know how to get out of it. Now it's going to be so embarrassing to admit that all these administrations have told so many untruths, it would be embarrassing getting out of it. There are a number of extraterrestrial vehicles out there cruising around."

–Gordon Cooper, Former NASA Astronaut, Aeronautical Engineer and test pilot. One of the seven original Astronauts in Project Mercury, the first manned space program of the United States

If we are right in our assumption that there is a Splinter Civilization—an elite offshoot of humanity that has kept incredible secrets and hoarded advanced technologies—then *Area 51* is one of the red flags signaling its existence.

After decades of denials and calling all conspiracy theorists deluded, the US Government has finally admitted the infamous Area 51, in the Nevada desert, *does* exist.

The top secret Cold War test site adjoining Nellis Air Force Base, northwest of Las Vegas, has long been fodder for speculation that the authorities have covered up reported sightings of UFO's and aliens. Until recently the government has denied its existence.

Now a newly declassified CIA document confirms the existence of Area 51. The document states the contentious zone was used as a testing range for the government's U-2 spy plane during the Cold War.

However, there's no mention of the controversial Roswell incident, which UFO believers claim was an alien space ship that crashed in New Mexico in 1947 and not a weather balloon as the authorities insisted. Supporters of the theory allege that Area 51's hangars were used to hide evidence of alien bodies recovered from the spaceship.

The CIA asserts government secrecy surrounding Area 51 was simply about ensuring

Above: An Area 51 warning sign

*"Area-51" by Ivank888—Own work.
Licensed under CC BY-SA 3.0 via Wikimedia Commons*

Above: An aerial photograph of Area 51

Area 51 28 August 1968 / 7
Via Wikimedia Commons

a new spy plane—the U-2 reconnaissance aircraft—remained hidden from prying Soviet eyes. Plausible considering the aircraft was designed specifically for high altitude snooping on the Soviets.

The agency's report explains the "tremendous increase in reports of unidentified flying objects" as an "unexpected side effect" of high altitude testing of the U-2. This increase was due to the aircraft's silver wings reflecting the rays of the sun, according to the official explanation.

However, this doesn't explain the interrelated Roswell incident or the many reported UFO, and indeed alien, sightings in and around Area 51 over the years.

It's easy to dismiss such sightings as the ramblings of zealous conspiracy theorists. However, in the wake of the US Government's belated and officialadmission that Area 51 does exist, maybe those reports shouldn't be dismissed quite so readily.

"You know, there aren't six people in this room who know how true this really is."

–President Ronald Reagan.
Conversation with Steven Spielberg at the White House on June 27, 1982 during a Presidential screening of
E.T. the Extra-Terrestrial.

We visit Area 51 and Nellis Air Force Base in our conspiracy thriller novel *The Orphan Uprising*. Our research for that novel raised more questions than answers—questions we'll probably never know the answers to.

Of all the explanations those in the conspiracy community want regarding Area 51, probably the most pressing is whether the global elite are housing *human* or *alien* technologies there.

If either was admitted to, that would be equally extraordinary.

Say what?

Well, if the anti-gravity flying machines witnessed by so many in and around Area 51's airspace are manmade then that confirms the Splinter Civilization are almost light years ahead of known science—and they have technologies the common man could scarcely comprehend.

If on the other hand UFO's are of alien origin, that implies the global elite are collaborating with an ET civilization—and this may explain why classified technology has progressed at such a rapid rate since around the time of Roswell.

Above: Are the UFO's seen around Area 51 manmade or ET tech?

*Alien spaceship breaking through the clouds over a desert highway
by Andrés Nieto Porras. Licensed under CC BY-SA 2.0 via Wikimedia Commons*

"There is abundant evidence that we are being contacted, that civilizations have been visiting us for a very long time. That their appearance is bizarre from any type of traditional materialistic western point of view. That these visitors use the technologies of consciousness, they use toroids, they use co-rotating magnetic disks for their propulsion systems, that seems to be a common denominator of the UFO phenomenon."

–Dr Brian O'Leary, Former NASA Astronaut and Princeton Physics Professor

As mentioned, for decades Area 51 was said to exist only in the furtive and skeptical minds of conspiracy theorists. Then Russian satellite photos of the facility were leaked and shared far and wide online. But still the US Government continued to maintain there was *no such place as Area 51* and blamed conspiracy theorists as being responsible for *spreading lies*.

Each and every US administration maintained this position until August 16, 2013 . . .

That was a day independent UFO researchers finally felt vindicated, for on that date the world's media reported that the CIA had officially announced the existence of Area 51.

This significant acknowledgement came by way of declassified documents procured via a public records request lodged by George Washington University's National Security Archive. The documentation included a CIA history of Area 51's top secret U-2 spy plane program. Where references to Area 51 had been redacted in earlier documentation released by the CIA, it was named for all to see in the latest documents.

In the outpouring of media commentary that followed, a ForeignPolicy.com editorial piece sums up the revelations better than most—describing Area 51 as "a touchstone of America's cultural mythology."

The editorial continues:

"It (Area 51) rose to notoriety in 1989, when a Las Vegas man claimed he had worked at the secret facility to discover the secrets of crashed alien hardware, spawning two decades of conspiracy theories and speculation about little green men. But the facility's history—and the history of the strange, secret aircraft that were developed there—extends back to 1955. Since its inception, the government has obliquely acknowledged its existence only a handful of times, and even the CIA's 1996 declassified history of the OXCART program—the development of the SR-71 Blackbird at the secret site—refers only to tests conducted in "the Nevada desert." The government has never publicly discussed the specific facility . . . until now."

Above: Top-secret black triangular craft on an unknown military runway in the United States

While the declassified documents acknowledge the Nevada site was a testing ground for surveillance during the Cold War, conspiracy theorists will be disappointed there's no mention of UFO's or aliens.

UFO sightings and conspiracy theories have dogged Area 51 since its inception. Time travel, advanced weapons programs and enormous underground bases, as well as the recovery of downed alien spacecraft and interaction with the occupants of those craft are just some of claims made by conspiracy theorists.

Of all the interrelated conspiracy claims surrounding Area 51, one stands out above all others: Roswell.

3

ROSWELL

"Yes there have been crashed craft, and bodies recovered.
We are not alone in the universe, they have been coming
here for a long time."

*–Dr. Edgar Mitchell, Astronaut and Lunar Module Pilot
(Apollo 14 Moon Landing)*

The *Roswell event* occurred near Roswell,
New Mexico, in 1947, when a mystery craft
crashed on a ranch and debris was recovered.
That much at least is true. The official
explanation—courtesy of the United States
Armed Forces—is the debris was the result of a

secret US military Air Force surveillance balloon crashing.

Interestingly, the very first official explanation—issued by an Army spokesman—was that the mystery craft was "a flying disc." That was quickly *corrected* in an Air Force statement advising that Roswell Army Air Field personnel had recovered a downed weather balloon at the crash site.

However, it's the unofficial explanations that most interest us. They obviously interest a lot of others, too: the public at large have been intrigued by the enduring theories the incident spawned—the most prominent being that the mystery craft was in fact a spaceship and that it contained extraterrestrial life.

A 1995 feature-length doco titled *The Roswell Incident* provides a compelling overview of the event, inclusive of very persuasive eye-witness accounts. At the time of writing, it's accessible via Top Documentary Films' website.

Top Documentary Films' splurge for the doco begins:

"In the summer of 1947, there were a number of UFO sightings in the United States. Sometime during the first week of July 1947, something crashed near Roswell.

"W.W. (Mack) Brazel, a New Mexico rancher, saddled up his horse and rode out with the son

Above: Photograph of a supposed alien Roswell survivor

"Ebe 1" by Unknown
Licensed under Public Domain via Wikimedia Commons

Above: An artist's recreation of the Roswell crash site

Roswell (reconstitution)
Licensed under Public Domain via Wikimedia Commons

of neighbors Floyd and Loretta Proctor, to check on the sheep after a fierce thunderstorm the night before. As they rode along, Brazel began to notice unusual pieces of what seemed to be metal debris, scattered over a large area. Upon further inspection, Brazel saw that a shallow trench, several hundred feet long, had been gouged into the land."

The doco reports the crash site was quickly sealed off by the military, but not before the discovery of four alien bodies outside a damaged spacecraft—at a second crash site— that was largely intact.

Sounds far-fetched? Many think so. Even a few high profile UFO commentators dismiss the Roswell-related alien body claims as implausible.

Then again, it's one of the oldest conspiracy theories around and it shows no sign of going away any time soon. One reason for this could be the eyewitnesses who claim, or claimed, to have observed the aftermath of the crash are in the main very credible and convincing.

"For some years I have had good reason to believe that world governments, headed by the Americans, not only have contact with alien races, but have reciprocal agreements with them, allowing certain species to come and go around our planet without hindrance."

–Tony Dodd. Former British police officer

Above: July 8, 1947 edition of the Roswell Daily Record
detailing the UFO incident

*Roswell Daily Record July,1947" by drew peacock
Licensed under Public Domain via Wikimedia Commons*

In fairness, it should be noted there are other conspiracy theories about the Roswell incident that have nothing whatsoever to do with aliens. One involves Japan and the aftermath of World War Two.

This version of Roswell, which apparently had many credible witnesses as well, insists that US military personnel did indeed find a crashed UFO with survivors aboard. However, the crucial difference compared to other Roswell reports is that military personnel claimed the survivors were not extraterrestrials but Japanese *people*.

The suggestion is the Japanese had access to their own antigravity propulsion technology – either manmade or extraterrestrial in origin – and they were planning to attack the US using advanced flying craft to avenge the atomic destruction of Hiroshima and Nagasaki in 1945.

Whether this story was a result of post war propaganda or paranoia on behalf of US military personnel, or whether the Japanese really did have antigravity propulsion systems of their own and were looking to exact justice, is anybody's guess.

Many who believe the Roswell crash survivors were Japanese and not extraterrestrials claim the popular ET conspiracy theories were purposefully leaked to journalists by the US Government. The aim, they say, was to conceal the Japanese attack and, more importantly, their exotic technologies, which the military felt needed to be kept hidden from the American public.

Several UFO researchers and independent Roswell investigators have written about these counter theories involving Japan and believe them to be true, or at least treat them very seriously. For example, the 2005 book *Body Snatchers in the Desert: The Horrible Truth at the Heart of the Roswell Story,* by Nick Redfern, emphatically states there were never any dead alien bodies.

"The crash-site discovery of prototype military aircraft would expose a damning secret," the intriguing book's synopsis states, "a highly confidential, U.S. government-sanctioned program to conduct medical experiments on deformed, handicapped, disfigured, and diseased Japanese POWs, exploited as "expendable" victims by their captors."

The book contains quotes from various government insiders including one female whistleblower known only as the *Black Widow* who apparently worked at the Oak Ridge National Laboratory, a classified military facility in Tennessee, from the mid-1940's until the early 1950's. She claims to have seen the deformed bodies of human subjects and

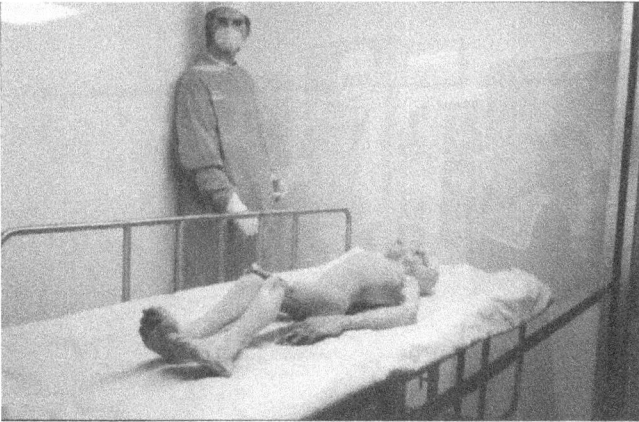

Above: Alien corpse dummy at the Roswell UFO Museum

*"Roswell UFO Museum (5527823449)" by InSapphoWeTrust from Los Angeles, California, USA
Roswell UFO Museum Uploaded by russavia
Licensed under CC BY-SA 2.0 via Wikimedia Commons*

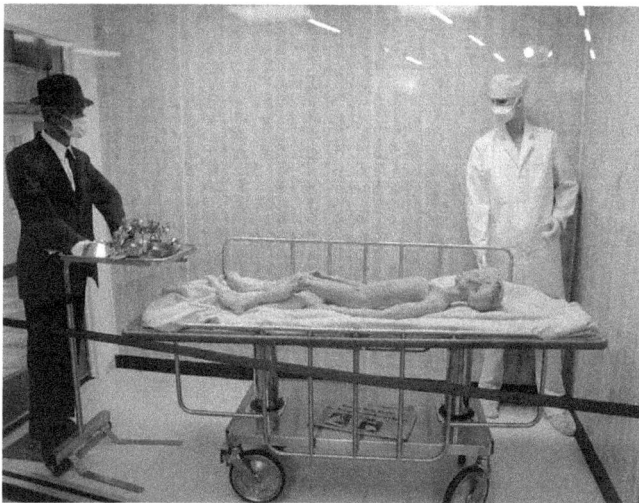

Above: Dramatization of a rumored alien autopsy

"Alien Autopsy–21 (4470867097)" by Jim Trottier from Kenosha, USA
Alien Autopsy–21 Uploaded by LongLiveRock
Licensed under CC BY-SA 2.0 via Wikimedia Commons

categorically stated they were all Japanese and that none were alien beings.

The Black Widow also claims the Japanese people had been captured after some kind of crash and had been used for biological and nuclear experiments at the White Sands missile range in southern New Mexico. She's quoted as saying, "All of the bodies were Oriental and around five feet in height . . . several exhibited signs of severe physical handicaps—such as oversized heads and malformed faces and hands—while others had slightly larger and protruding eyes."

Author Nick Redfern also writes about several other whistleblowers in his book. They include: an individual named Levine who worked for the British Government's Home Office and confirmed the stories of alien bodies were totally false; another Oak Ridge insider who claimed the recovered bodies were of Asian origins; a former DIA agent known as *the Colonel* who claimed to have knowledge of the experimental flying machines in New Mexico at the time and also said that one of his jobs at the DIA was to send out "false UFO stories to the Russians, to the Communists" and also distribute false "sightings of flying saucer landings at military facilities, stories that we had crashed UFOs and bodies of space aliens."

Army Reveals It Has Flying Disc Found On Ranch In New Mexico

ROSWELL, (N. M.), July 8.— (P)—The army air forces here today announced a flying disc has been found on a ranch near Roswell and is in possession of the army. Lieutenant Warren Haught, public information officer of the Roswell Army Air Field, announced the find had bee made "sometime last week" and had been turned over to the air field through cooperation of the sheriff's office.

Higher Headquarters

"It was inspected at the Roswell Army Air Field and subsequently loaned" by Major Jesse A. Marcell of the 409th Bomb Group intelligence officer in Roswell "to higher headquarters."

The army gave no other details.

Above: Newspaper clipping from the Sacramento Bee—July 8, 1947

Redfern, a Brit living in Texas and a best-selling author and journalist, is probably one of the more savvy researchers to investigate the Roswell incident. In forming his hypothesis about the 1947 incident while writing *Body Snatchers in the Desert,* he accessed thousands of US Government archive documents as well gaining direct access to insiders in British intelligence.

Therefore, his non-extraterrestrial explanation for Roswell cannot be easily dismissed.

Could it really be that most UFO investigators are deceived in their notions about Roswell? Or were alien bodies really found at the mysterious crash site as per the more popular conspiracy theory?

Almost 70 years after the Roswell incident, the public and most independent investigators generally seem to be none the wiser.

One thing's for sure, no smoking gun has been found and hard evidence to support the presence of either alien, Japanese or other human bodies is lacking. Much like the JFK assassination, there are now so many theories and counter theories floating around about Roswell that the truth may never be known.

4

· · · ● ● ● ● ● ● · · ·

AREA 51 ACCOUNTS FROM INSIDERS

"Behind the scenes, high ranking Air Force officers are soberly concerned about UFOs. But through official secrecy and ridicule, many citizens are led to believe the unknown flying objects are nonsense."

- Roscoe H. Hillenkoetter, Former Director of the CIA, 1960.

Numerous insiders from the US military and intelligence communities have stated that the technologies at Area 51 are of extraterrestrial origins. These individuals are, or were, for the most part former military employees, and in many cases they died after giving testimony!

Coincidences perhaps?

Probably the best known of these insiders is one Bob Lazar who claims he was employed as a scientist in the late 1980's to study recovered ET technologies housed at a top-secret facility known as *S4,* which is said to be in, or bordering, Area 51.

Lazar, who is an electronics expert and a former document photo processor, says he had to pass strict military tests before being permitted to study the recovered ET craft. His assignment was to determine how humans could fly the craft and how more such craft could be constructed.

The scientist claims the craft he studied had extraordinary super physics abilities. It could bend the fabric of space and time, thereby making it capable of defying Einstein's *Theory of Relativity* by teleporting and time traveling.

After studying the first craft, Lazar says he was put to work on other spacecraft. Yes you read that right: *other spacecraft.*

In total, over the 12 months Lazar worked at Area 51, he claims he experimented with nine different extraterrestrial vehicles. Apparently these craft used a unique fuel—one that Lazar called *Element 115*—that allowed the Beings

Above: Bob Lazar

"Bob-Lazar" by Dudeanatortron—Own work.
Licensed under CC BY-SA 4.0 via Wikimedia Commons

Above: Film still of unnamed dying CIA agent
(now presumed dead)

who created them to travel across the universe at or somewhere near the speed of light.

Potentially supporting Lazar's testimonial, Element 115 was discovered on August 28, 2013, prompting various news outlets and scientific journals to run stories on the discovery that same day. These included an article by National Geographic headed *Meet 115, the Newest Element on the Periodic Table.* It mentions how the "extremely heavy element was just confirmed by scientists in Sweden."

UFO website openminds.tv also posted an article the same day, mentioning Lazar's claim of 23 years earlier. "Element 115 received attention in 1989 when Area 51 whistleblower Bob Lazar asserted that extraterrestrial spacecraft at Area 51's S4 facility were powered by the element."

Another intriguing case is the deathbed testimonial of an ex-CIA employee who convincingly reveals what he insists is the truth regarding extraterrestrials' involvement with humanity. The recorded interview was conducted by US television host and respected UFO author Richard Dolan, and filmed on March 5, 2013 at an undisclosed location somewhere in mainland America.

The dying man, who remained unnamed presumably to protect his family, claims to have been hired by the CIA when he was a young man in the 1950's. He says he was first employed to investigate UFO's in the top-secret *Project Blue Book,* another former conspiracy theory which has since been proven to be legitimate in the light of declassified CIA documents.

The elderly gentleman, who—unless he's the world's greatest actor—was clearly on his deathbed, also speaks of being sent to Area 51 on behalf of President Eisenhower where he not only witnessed ET antigravity technologies, but also says he met a real, live Grey Alien.

A May 3, 2013 article, again on the *Open Minds* UFO investigation website, accurately summarizes the aforementioned interview— referring to the unnamed interview subject as 'Anonymous'—(abridged) as follows: "Facing impending kidney failure, this individual felt compelled to disclose secret information he feels is too important to keep secret . . . 'Anonymous' alleges that, after an invasion threat . . . President Dwight Eisenhower, he and his superior at the CIA were allowed inside the secretive Area 51 in Nevada to gather intel and report back to the president. There, 'Anonymous' describes seeing several alien spacecraft, including the craft that crashed in Roswell, New Mexico. Then, he and his superior were taken to the S-4 facility southwest of Area 51 where they observed live extraterrestrials."

Footage of the testimonial was first shown to the public on May 3, 2013 at the Citizen Hearing on Disclosure, at the National Press Club, in Washington, DC.

UFO researcher and bestselling author Peter Robbins, who attended the Citizen Hearing, watched the recorded testimony at that event.

Robbins wrote the following on his Facebook account after the screening: "In my opinion, if it can be confirmed by any relevant supporting documentation, this moving and fascinating account does qualify as an authentic 'death bed' testimony from an individual who convincingly claims to have been a CIA officer deeply involved in the matter of crashed and/or recovered craft, and at one time a liaison between the Agency and the President."

The filmed testimonial has since been uploaded by various YouTube users and has been watched by millions of people, prompting many to comment that their "gut feelings" tell them the elderly gent is telling the truth, and also that it would be very hard to fake being that sick. Although some think it's a fabrication, the consensus—judging by comments left below the uploaded versions of the testimonial—supports the unnamed man's testimonial.

Finally, it should be noted that the testimonial, which has not yet been verified as either true or false, dovetails with a long-held popular theory which suggests the US Government entered into an agreement with an

ET civilization. According to this theory, a deal was struck up with President Eisenhower and these other Beings whereby the US would be the beneficiaries of their advanced technologies provided the ET's could visit the US and elsewhere on Planet Earth at will to carry out whatever their agenda may be.

Some conspiracy theorists say that alien agenda includes abducting humans. Interestingly, the self-proclaimed former CIA agent who gave the deathbed testimonial also mentions that Eisenhower agreed to allow the aliens to abduct humans, including US citizens, as part of the agreement he signed with them.

5

···•••●●●•••··

CLOSE ENCOUNTERS OF THE FOURTH KIND

"In our obsession with antagonisms of the moment, we often forget how much unites all the members of humanity. Perhaps we need some outside, universal threat to make us recognize this common bond. I occasionally think how quickly our differences worldwide would vanish if we were facing an alien threat from outside of this world. And yet I ask—is not an alien force already among us?"

–President Ronald Reagan at the UN General Assembly. September 21, 1987, Geneva, Switzerland.

In this book's Introduction, you'll recall we warned that we would at times go slightly off-topic into areas that don't strictly relate to the classified space exploration technology this book is about.

Well, this chapter is *the* big tangent we previously alluded to.

However, we trust you will come to the conclusion we reached—that the following is crucial to piecing together what this UFO technology is and where it comes from.

So even though what follows does not directly relate to antigravity propulsion, we would be remiss not to discuss alien abductees—those who have been abducted by aliens or those who *imagine* they have depending on your take—in this book.

After all, the main question we are exploring here is: are all reports of flying saucers the result of alien or human technologies?

Although we haven't devoted much time to researching abductees' claims, we have by chance been personally involved with one of the most incredible and supposedly true accounts of alien abduction ever told.

Around 2005–2006, we took out an option to the film rights of the 1998 book *Coevolution: The True Story of a Man Taken for Ten Days to an Extraterrestrial Civilization,* by fellow New Zealander Alec Newald whom we interviewed at

Above: Artistic depiction of an alien abduction by Travis Walton

"Walton(reconstitution)" by Own work.
Licensed under Public Domain via Wikimedia Commons

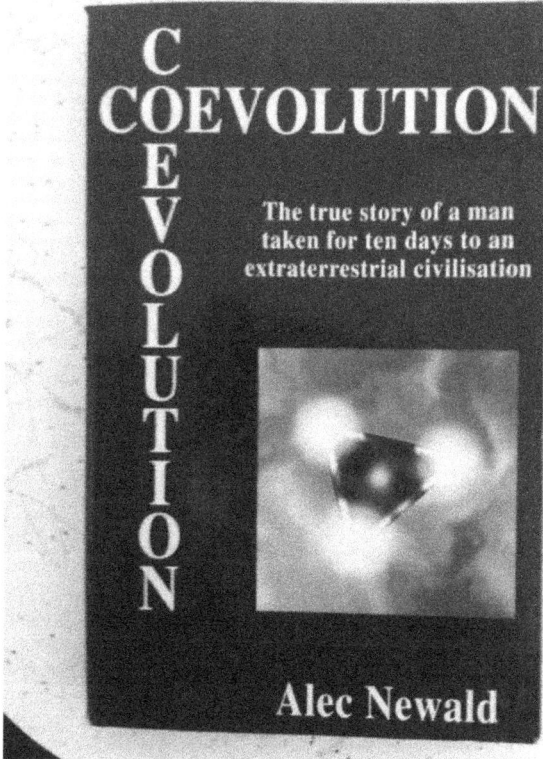

Above: The book cover of COEVOLUTION

length and subsequently wrote a treatment for a feature film screenplay adaptation of his book.

We believed the planned film would take the alien and space genres to a whole new level. Unfortunately, scheduling conflicts with our filmmaking slates prevented us from devoting the time required to produce the movie.

As the book's full title suggests, *Coevolution* is about *The True Story of a Man Taken for Ten Days to an Extraterrestrial Civilization*. Here is the book's blurb sourced from the popular reading social network Goodreads.com:

"One Monday in mid-February 1989, Alec Newald set off on what should have been a three-hour drive from Rotorua to Auckland, New Zealand. Instead he became a missing person for ten days. Newald claims that during those ten days he was taken by friendly aliens to their home planet, which he describes in full and awesome detail (for) part of this book—an amazing first-person account of a growing but still unexplained phenomenon."

Alec writes at length in the book how after being returned to Earth he was mysteriously contacted by agents of unnamed international intelligence agencies, even though he'd told nobody about his alien abduction. These agents harassed, threatened and tortured Alec in their belief he wasn't divulging all the information he had about this ET civilization. They also advised him he would, in the interests of self-preservation, be best to never publicly divulge what he experienced or mention the *technologies* he'd witnessed.

But that didn't deter Alec, who describes himself as a stubborn individual; he subsequently wrote the book about his other worldly experience.

Coevolution contains detailed drawings of the friendly ET's he claims he met, as well as sketches of their spacecraft, their advanced technologies and the planet they took him to. He also has in his possession crystals and other rock formations he says he brought back from the planet.

Above: Alec Newald

We had no way of verifying this, but the rocks were strange and like none we'd seen. Of course, we were essentially approaching the planned film adaptation from a storytellers' perspective—meaning we believed it would make a very entertaining movie, and didn't give a lot of thought as to how likely it was true.

What we can say is Alec, who is a professional sailmaker by trade, believes 100% this happened to him. As an apparently sane and balanced individual, he presents a very convincing case. However, in considering such extraordinary claims, we must remember the mind is a very complex thing; its workings can deceive even the most stable individual, especially in times of stress or other outward influences.

Worth noting, especially for sci-fi fans, is Alec's claim that we humans are the ancestors of aliens and they, in turn, are our descendants from the future who have mastered time travel. Apparently, the ET's Alec befriended are close to extinction as a result of decisions their ancestors (we Earthlings!) made. They therefore regularly time travel back into their past to positively influence present-day humanity so they can improve their own reality.

And on top of all those complexities, Alec also recounts in his book a love affair with one of the female aliens whom he describes as having out-of-this-world beauty—figuratively and literally!

As filmmakers, we felt *Coevolution* would make an explosive and contentious sci-fi movie worthy of a Steven Spielberg blockbuster. We still feel that way. It's our hope that either a feature film or at the very least a feature-length documentary on it is eventually produced, exploring the mystery of Alec Newald's missing 10 days in the year 1989.

"There is a serious possibility that we are being visited and have been visited for many years by people from outer space, by other civilizations. Who they are, where they are from, and what they want should be the subject of rigorous scientific investigation and not be the subject of 'rubbishing' by tabloid newspapers."

—Lord Admiral Hill-Norton, former Head of the British Ministry of Defense and Chairman of the NATO Military Committee

The other key alien encounter report worth mentioning is the curious case of American Philip Schneider (1947–1996).

Schneider's story is one of the most out-there, yet hard-to-dismiss testimonials supporting the existence of underground bases and the rumored ET's some of them hide—not to mention the advanced technologies housed in these subterranean military facilities.

Although very few records exist on the man and his military career, Schneider stated he was a geologist and former government military engineer. More controversially, he also claimed to have been involved in a firefight that broke out with extraterrestrials while he was building

Friday November 21, 2014   **05**

mX NEWS

●ET TALKS

Invaded by alien theories

Lauren McMah

The person sitting next to you could well be an extraterrestrial.

So says US-based conspiracy theorist Kerry Cassidy, who is in town for talks at Waterloo's dMBUSH Gallery this weekend.

"They (ETs) have chosen in many cases to deal one-on-one with people around the world, or to go out en masse, and they're also dealing with different secret governments and treaties that they set up with them that allow them to do what they want to do," she told mX.

"I'm fascinated by ETs that are visiting Earth and the different cultures and different kinds of beings that we're dealing with, both on and off the planet and from underground.

"I think we've only grazed the surface as humans in understanding the multidimensional qualities of our world."

Like a real-life Fox Mulder from TV's The X-Files, Cassidy has spent years interviewing whistleblowers around the world on all manner of subjects, from alien conspiracies to government cover-ups.

She will discuss these "truths", along with her experiences with whistleblowers, during her talks along with 17 contemporary artists.

"The bottom line is to wake the world up to what we can show beyond the matrix. To change their perception of reality, so they can take that with them and further investigate, learn on their own, and take it from there," Cassidy said.

See rmbushgallery.com

Above: Article about ETs in Sydney's daily newspaper MX

Above: Film still of Philip Schneider shortly before he died

additions to the underground military base at Dulce, New Mexico, in 1979.

Schneider said he was one of only three survivors in the humans versus aliens battle in which 66 US Delta Force soldiers were killed. Although Schneider survived, he had severe flesh wounds and burns to his entire body—wounds he claimed were the result of some kind of radiation weapon the ET's fired at him.

In the mid-1990's, Schneider began giving lectures all over the world about what he said was the absolute truth regarding ET's living below Earth's surface. During one such lecture, at the Preparedness Expo in November of 1995, he said, "Right now military technology is about 1200 years more advanced than public state technology."

During another lecture, Schneider mentioned how in 1954 the Eisenhower administration disregarded the Constitution by signing a treaty with the ET's. The treaty was apparently named *The 1954 Greada Treaty*.

In the same lecture, he mentioned a human-looking alien who was "one of the aliens who has been working for the Pentagon for the last 58 years." He then produced a photograph of this supposed alien and showed it to the audience and the cameraman filming the lecture.

Providing a possible insight into the Splinter Civilization's monetary resources, Schneider claimed that since the 1940's the US Government had spent almost *one quadrillion dollars* building hundreds of underground bases all over America.

In the course of delivering these lectures—some of which were filmed and are available for anyone to see on the Internet—Schneider displayed visible injuries, including missing fingers and chest wounds, which he claimed were a legacy of the battle with the ET's. To back up his statements, Schneider also produced what he claimed were classified photographs, ancient alien fossils and non-Earth metal ores retrieved from Dulce Base.

In his last recorded lecture, Schneider told his audience there had been 13 murder attempts on his life by government agents intent on preventing him continuing to inform the public of the existence of ET's. He said he was speaking out because, "I love my country more than I love my own life."

Schneider was found dead in his apartment in Wilsonville, Oregon, on January 17, 1996, several days after he'd died.

As with everything else in Schneider's life, his death was also shrouded in mystery. Initially, the Clackamas County Coroner's office said he'd died of either a stroke or a heart attack. Then they changed their story to suicide.

It's also worth noting that all the geologist's documents relating to underground bases, as well as the alleged alien artifacts that he'd begun showing to audiences, went missing and have never been seen since.

Cynthia Drayer, Schneider's ex-wife, is one of many who firmly believe Schneider was murdered to prevent him from leaking anything more about the ET-human interactions occurring below ground.

As one would expect, without undeniable evidence or absolute proof left behind to confirm Schneider's story, there are as many skeptics as believers. The former include some who insist they've debunked all his claims about underground bases and ET's.

On the other hand, it could reasonably be argued undeniable evidence is exceedingly difficult to obtain when it comes to proving the Splinter Civilization exists and is in our midst— not to mention proving that alien civilizations have already arrived on Earth.

"It followed us during half of our orbit. We observed it on the light side, and when we entered the shadow side, it disappeared completely. It was an engineered structure,

made from some type of metal, approximately 40 meters long with inner hulls. The object was narrow here and wider here, and inside there were openings. Some places had projections like small wings. The object stayed very close to us. We photographed it, and our photos showed it to be 23 to 28 meters away."

—Cosmonaut Victor Afanasyev commenting on a UFO sighting that occurred while en route to the Solyut 6 space station in April of 1979.

6

· · · • ● ⬤ ● • · ·

THE CASE FOR MANMADE TECHNOLOGIES

"I heard you had reports this morning of an unidentified aircraft. Don't worry it was just me."

–George W. Bush speaking to the Military Academy in Roswell, New Mexico, January 22, 2004

There's no denying the Roswell event unearthed some convincing *evidence* and very credible eye witnesses, and there have been innumerable reported UFO sightings from around the world since that incident.

A likely explanation for those sightings in and around Area 51 air space in particular is that they are in fact manmade machines—such as the once-secret U-2 spy plane—primarily originating in the Cold War in which America was a willing participant.

Since the U-2's development and subsequent *unveiling,* the public have become familiar with other cutting-edge aviation developments—such as the Stealth Bomber.

But what else *out there* is manmade?

Rumors of government-sponsored craft capable of traveling at unearthly speeds and resembling flying saucers have been around since World War Two. That includes the legendary Nazi *foo fighter* flying saucers, which scores of Allied pilots reported witnessing in-flight.

Given the many thousands of UFO reports logged around the world every year, such rumors shouldn't be dismissed too lightly. Certainly, manmade craft would be a more logical explanation for UFO sightings than alien craft. Not because it's unlikely there's life beyond our planet. Rather, because it could be argued it's unlikely other beings have discovered our little corner of the universe just yet.

This thinking suggests the odds of the Earth being discovered are astronomical given the size

Above: A painting depicting the history of NACA, NASA and futuristic developments

"Expanding the Frontiers of Flight" by NASA/ Robert McCall
Licensed under Public Domain via Wikimedia Commons

Above: Philip J. Corso (far right) receiving the Bronze Star in Rome, 1945

"Philip j corso 2" by US Army—US Army
Licensed under Public Domain via Wikimedia Commons

of our Universe. It's a rather large 28 billion light-years in diameter, according to scientists, although that doesn't take into account the Universe's expansion since this book underwent its final proofing.

Furthermore, if there's one thing our research has taught us, it is that it's naïve to believe *the latest* technology in the public domain is truly the latest. There are numerous examples of products or technology being introduced as new, or cutting-edge, whereas they had already been secretly used—for years or decades in many cases—by the military or by certain government agencies, or both. The Internet was one such case, first being used for a number of years by the military before eventually being released to the public.

If we can accept that, we should be able to accept that there are new technologies, both in development and in existence right now, the average person couldn't even begin to imagine.

This idea of futuristic science existing in the present as classified science is likely to be as true in earlier eras as it is today. Earlier eras that include the post-WW2 period of Roswell, according to many UFO researchers.

Researchers like Colonel Philip J. Corso, whose 1997 book *The Day After Roswell* does, in places, present convincing evidence to support the theory that antigravitational propulsion systems and related technologies could be manmade.

In fact, Colonel Corso is not so much a researcher but a Roswell insider who claims to have handled all the wreckage from the incident's crash site. Corso was a member of President Eisenhower's National Security Council and former head of the Foreign Technology Desk at the US Army's Research and Development department.

"As early as September 1947," the book states, "scientists who had gone to the Air Materiel Command at Wright Field to see the debris were speculating that the electronic potential of the Roswell craft reminded them of the German and British antigravity experiments of the 1920s and 1930s."

If the 1947 flying saucer crash debris stored at Wright-Patterson Air Force Base was strikingly reminiscent of earlier scientific theories, experiments or inventions, then it only seems logical to conclude that whatever the strange technology was at Roswell it did *not* come from some far away galaxy. Rather, the more plausible assumption would appear to be that the craft was entirely a product of Earthbound science, but *classified* science not known of by the general public.

Colonel Corso continues, "General Twining was reported to have said more than once that the name of the Serbian electrical engineer and inventor of alternating current, Nikola Tesla, kept bubbling up in the conversation because the scientists examining the damaged craft described the way it must have converted an electromagnetic field into an antigravity field. And, of course, the craft itself reminded them of the German experimental fighter aircraft that made their appearance near the end of the war but that had been in development ever since the 1930s."

Some pertinent observations were made about the *The Day After Roswell* by UFO researcher Michael Lindemann in an article he wrote for CNI News.

"In the course of describing his handling of the wreckage," Lindemann writes, "Corso makes numerous interesting side comments. For example, he says he soon realized that a small hand-held laser he found in the filing cabinet must be a surgical cutting instrument, which was probably used in cattle mutilations. He also says he learned that the Roswell UFO was "a delta-shaped object," a claim that fits recent speculations by Roswell researchers Randle and Schmitt and forensic investigator William McDonald."

Colonel Corso also mentions in his book other pre-WW2 experiments that allude to the potential of ordinary *human* science being capable of creating UFO-type crafts.

"If the magnetic field theory experiments carried out by engineers and electrical energy pioneers Paul Biefeld and Townsend Brown in the 1920s at the California Institute for Advanced Studies were accurately reported—and the U.S. military as well as scientific record keepers at the Bureau of Investigation kept very close tabs on what these engineers were doing—then the technological theory for antigravity flight existed before World War II."

Colonel Corso continues, "In fact, prototypes for vertical takeoff and landing disk shaped aircraft had been on the drawing boards at the California Institute since before the war. It was just that in the United States nobody paid them much attention. The Germans did develop and had flown flying disks, or so the intelligence reports read, even though they had no impact on the outcome of the war other than stimulating a race between the United States and the USSR to gather as much of the German technology as possible."

Many researchers, historians and scientists alike have postulated that the Nazis successfully developed antigravity technologies during or even before WW2—and as per Corso's aforementioned statements, US intelligence reports confirm this.

As Nick Cook mentions in his 2007 non-fiction title *The Hunt for Zero Point: Inside the Classified World of Antigravity Technology,*

Above: Could Nikola Tesla's revolutionary science have resulted in manmade UFO's?

"Tesla3" by Napoleon Sarony—postcard 1890, scanned from my collection in 2007 cropped from: image:Tesla2.jpg. Licensed under Public Domain via Wikimedia Commons

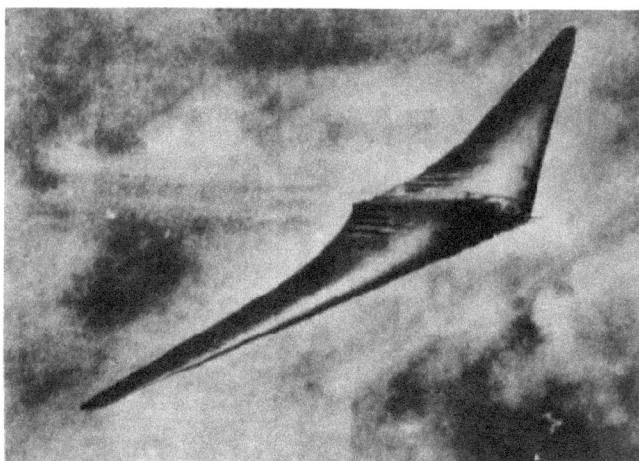

Above: Anonymous image of advanced Nazi fighter plane

there seems to be ample evidence to show flying saucer technology was indeed developed by the Nazis during the war. In his book, Cook mentions Polish researcher Igor Witkowski, who apparently discovered evidence of a secret Nazi antigravity project.

Witkowski informed Cook of a strange Nazi experiment known simply as *The Bell*. And, in *The Hunt for Zero Point,* Cook informs readers about Witkowski's discoveries.

"A series of experiments had taken place in a mine in a valley close to the Czech frontier," according to Cook. "The experiments required large doses of electricity fed via thick cabling into a chamber hundreds of meters belowground. In this chamber, a bell-shaped device comprising two contra-rotating cylinders filled with mercury, or something like it, had emitted a strange pale blue light . . . A number of scientists who had been exposed to the device during these experiments suffered terrible side effects; five were said to have died as a result. Word had it that the tests sought to investigate some kind of anti-gravitational effect."

In other words, the Nazis were deep into developing antigravity propulsion systems aka flying saucers aka UFO's! And if the Nazis had such technologies, then the Allies (especially the United States) could have gained possession and control of them at the end of WW2 and begun developing antigravity flying machines in their own militaries.

It also appears there may once again exist a possible connection with Japan in regards to these technologies. Japanese scientist Dr. Takaaki Musha informed us of an interrelated UFO account during our research. The story concerns Dr. Musha's father, Haruo Musha (1924–2011).

"My father, Haruo, who was a military officer at the time of World War Two, told me that he was ordered to be trained in Manchukuo (the wartime Japanese-occupied Manchuria in Northern China) to become the pilot of a super advanced fighter plane delivered from Germany with other advanced technologies such as the atomic bomb. The Japanese Imperial Army had secret facilities there and developed weapons including advanced fighters."

Dr. Musha continues, "General Kanji Ishiwara, who established Manchukuo, had a plan to develop an advanced fighter which would be able to fly at high speed around the world without refueling. He wanted to prepare for the *last war* with the United States in Manchukuo.

"As a younger man, Ishiwara had studied in Germany and it is possible he connected with the Nazis at some point in his career and learnt

Above: A photo of unknown origins of a supposed Nazi flying saucer

Above: Kanji Ishiwara 1889–1949

about their antigravity technologies in active development."

It seems there could be some kind of connecting thread between the Nazis, the Japanese and the Roswell UFO crash.

To our way of thinking, when early-mid 20th Century science is analyzed in its totality, it will be obvious that science of that era had already evolved to the point where sophisticated antigravity UFO technologies could be built by Man. Obvious *clues* to support that assertion include the classified antigravity experiments conducted by the Nazis, British and Americans, and semi-secret (since classified) scientific experiments like those of Nikola Tesla's.

"We already have the means to travel among the stars, but these technologies are locked up in black projects, and it would take an act of God to ever get them out to benefit humanity. Anything you can imagine, we already know how to do."

–Ben Rich, former senior engineer in Lockheed Martin and former Director of Lockheed's advanced aerospace technology division Skunk Works.

7

· · · • • ● ● ● • • · ·

DISINFORMING THE PUBLIC

"I've been working with Paul Hellyer. He's the minister, the ex-minister of defense, Canada, under Trudeau. He is upset because the Americans are planning the weaponization of space, as though they (ET's) are enemies . . . It came out of a project called Project Paperclip, in which—and this is what Eisenhower warned us against—the sustention of the Military Industrial Complex. In order to extend the power and the funding of the Military Industrial Complex, you have to be afraid of things. Number one was communism. If that petered

out, number two is terrorism. That's here for a while. Number three is asteroids. And number four is extraterrestrials."

–Shirley MacLaine. Excerpt from an interview with Larry King on Larry King Live that aired on CNN on November 9, 2007.

Perhaps the ET and UFO movements are simply disinformation—i.e. deception, propaganda or half-truths.

Persuading everyone to believe in aliens compels us to look *up* to the skies. And while we are all waiting for *Little Green Men* to arrive, the shadowy people in the Splinter Civilization effortlessly go about their secret work by advancing their suppressed inventions at a rate of knots.

This disinformation counter-conspiracy theory suggests that, collectively, accounts of ET's coming, or crash-landing, or even living amongst us, conveniently form the perfect cover story. It's a story that is spread by intelligence agencies which encourage, and even surreptitiously finance, Hollywood film studios to make mega-budget movies about aliens and alien invasions.

Maybe the widespread acceptance by many that aliens have arrived on Earth at some point—or at least a willingness to consider such

Above: One of the mythological Little Green Men

"Alien2."
Licensed under Public Domain via Wikimedia Commons

Above: Is the film industry perpetuating myths about UFO's being ET crafts?

"Hollywood Sign" by Adrian104—Own work.
Licensed under Public Domain via Wikimedia Commons

a thing is possible—can be blamed on Hollywood. More likely, it can be attributed to the fact that we have been given so little of the big picture. (No pun intended).

If the Splinter Civilization's suppressed technologies were revealed in their entirety to the public at large, would everyone still believe UFO's *must be* of extraterrestrial origin?

Take Nikola Tesla's technologies alone. If these were suddenly declassified and opened up to public scrutiny, would we still be so quick to automatically assume that any alien civilization is superior, scientifically or otherwise, to our own? For all anyone knows, humanity may be the most scientifically advanced civilization in the entire universe.

"The phenomenon of UFOs does exist, and it must be treated seriously."

–Mikhail Gorbachev, 'Soviet Youth' speech, May 4, 1990.

Popular Culture's influence on Area 51 myths

The rumors swirling around Area 51 have given it a life of its own and have resulted in numerous films, TV programs, comics and video games.

Previously, these were readily identifiable as fiction because, for starters, they portrayed a place that didn't exist—not officially at least. We refer, of course, to Area 51.

However, now that we know for sure that Area 51 does exist and has existed all along, perhaps the likes of the 1994 TV movie *Roswell,* starring Martin Sheen, the Roland Emmerich-helmed *Independence Day,* starring Will Smith, and the Steven Spielberg-produced TV mini-series *Taken,* starring Dakota Fanning, will be viewed in a different light . . .

But are such dramatizations any closer to the truth than the stories government *spin merchants* have fed to us about UFO sightings these past decades? If there is a Splinter Civilization currently operating under the surface—both figuratively and literally—then perhaps it's not in the global elite's interests to shatter the ET myths perpetuated by conspiracy theorists and Hollywood film studios. Perhaps it serves the Splinter Civilization's agenda just fine.

8

· · · • • ● ● ● • • · ·

EINSTEIN'S UNIFIED FIELD THEORY

Strengthening the case for UFO's being manmade and of earthly origins, is the history of *electrogravitic propulsion.* It's a history that's either known, little known, rumored or usually unknown—depending on who you talk to.

According to American linguist and bestselling author Charles Berlitz, there was a rumor at Princeton's Institute for Advanced Study that Albert Einstein did indeed complete a version of his *Unified Field Theory for Gravitation and Electricity*—even though officially it remains a never-completed theory.

At first, this theory was published in German and appeared in a few scientific journals. In his papers, Einstein called his purported mathematical proof of the connection between the forces of electromagnetism and gravity as being "highly convincing."

However, this work was withdrawn as incomplete, although no published reason is given save that Einstein suddenly grew dissatisfied with it.

British mathematician Lord Bertrand Russell considered Einstein's *Unified Field Theory* complete, but felt that "Man is not ready for it and shan't be until after World War III."

Thus the Unified Field Theory on the connection between gravity and the electromagnetic field has remained unproven.

Leading scientist and former high-ranking employee of Japan's Ministry of Defense, Dr. Takaaki Musha, published an article in the 2004, Issue 53 edition of the *Infinite Energy Magazine* relating to this very question. The article, which covers a unique formula Dr. Musha developed for the link between electromagnetism and gravitation, was titled *The possibility of strong coupling between electricity and gravitation.*

After publication of the article, Dr. Musha claims he was contacted by Doctor (name redacted) from the Institute for Nuclear

The Possibility of Strong Coupling Between Electricity and Gravitation

Takaaki Musha*

Editor's Note: The paper is noteworthy, apart from its theoretical proposal, in revealing experimental work conducted at the Honda Corporation Research Institute in 1996.—EPM

Abstract
The finding of Prof. Biefeld and T.T. Brown, which is called the Biefeld-Brown effect, suggests strong coupling between electricity and gravitation. However, this phenomenon can not be predicted within the framework of conventional physics. The author attempts to explain this phenomenon by introducing an asymmetrical gravitational field generated inside the atom by a high potential electric field; he also verifies the theoretical value compared with the experimental result.

Introduction
Prof. Biefeld and T.T. Brown discovered that a high potential charged capacitor with dielectrics exhibited unidirectional thrust toward the positive plate when the atoms of a material are placed within the electric field of a capacitor. This phenomenon is called the Biefeld-Brown effect (B-B effect) and it suggests a connection between electricity and gravitation.

Characteristics of the B-B effect can be summarized shown as follows:[1]

1) The separation of the plates of the condenser—closer plates, greater effect.

2) The higher the specific inductive capacity of the dielectrics between the plates, the greater the effect.

3) The greater the area of the condenser plates, the greater the effect.

4) The greater the voltage difference between the plates, the greater the effect.

5) The greater the mass of the material between the plates, the greater the effect.

However, the coupling between electrostatic and gravitational fields can be predicted neither by General Relativity, nor conventional field theory. The author attempts to explain this phenomenon by introducing a new gravitational field generated inside the atom by a high potential electric field.

Theoretical Consideration on the B-B Effect
Weak field approximation of Einstein's General Relativity leads to the generalized formula of Lorentz force given by[2]

$$F = q(E + v \times B) + m(E_g + v \times B_g), \qquad (1)$$

where q is the charge of the particle, m is the mass of the particle, E is the electric field, B is the magnetic field, v is the velocity of the particle, E_g is the electrogravitic field, and B_g is the magnetogravitic field.

From which, gravitoelectric-electric coupling inside the static atom under high electric potential field becomes

$$qE + mE_g = 0, \qquad (2)$$

by assuming that the internal volume of an elementary particle is a region of force-free field like a superconductor.[3] Then the gravitational field generated at the center of the charged particle by an external electric field becomes

$$E_g = -(q/m)E. \qquad (3)$$

Comparing q/m values of an electron and a pion, E_g can be generated by an electron rather than a pion, hence we can let $q = e$ and $m = m_e$, where e is a charge of an electron and m_e is its mass. For the estimation of gravitational effect, we introduce the following approximation of the electrogravitic potential given by

$$\Phi_g = -(e/m_e)\theta\{\delta^2 x/(b^2 + x^2)\}, \qquad (4)$$

which satisfies the following conditions:

$$\partial \Phi_g(0) / \partial x = -(e/m_e)E. \qquad (5.1)$$

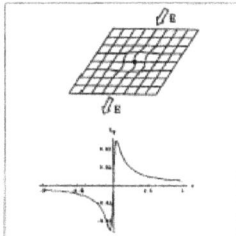

Figure 1. New gravitational field generated by an external electric field

Above: Dr. Musha's paper on Infinite Energy

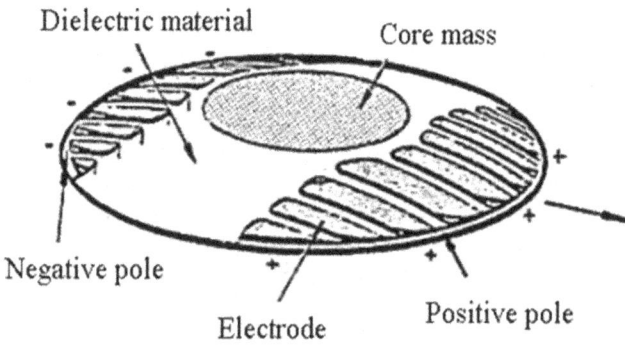

Above: Diagram of Electrogravitic craft by T.T. Brown

Research and Nuclear Energy, in Bulgaria. The Bulgarian scientist, whose name we have withheld due to our inability to reach him for comment before this book's publication, was already working on a similar formula to Dr. Musha's.

According to Dr. Musha, the Bulgarian's "formulation proves it is possible to create an unbalanced acceleration by creating intense electric and magnetic fields in a dielectric or ferromagnetic medium. These predicted coupling effects for electromagnetic and gravitational fields would be static and thus they should be able to produce a net force to *propel a spaceship.*"

The Bulgarian scientist wrote two papers on his formula in 1994.

"However," Dr. Musha claims, these "papers were rejected by two well-known science journals."

The strong implication is there was a cover-up. Either that or mainstream science was just not prepared to consider such theories on antigravity.

T. T. Brown, who discovered this electrogravitic effect first, conducted several experiments during the 1950's and succeeded to generate thrust without the reliance on a surrounding medium, such as air, by applying high voltages to materials with high dielectric constants. Around this time, US aerospace companies also become involved in such research, but their results are mostly classified.

In the late 1980's and early 1990's, a rash of observer *sightings* of unidentified, high-speed, high-flying air vehicles continued, but the US Government repeatedly denied it had developed an aircraft to replace the Mach 3-plus Lockheed SR-71 strategic reconnaissance platform—indicating it (the government) was content to let the public assume the sightings were of the SR-71.

In the 1990's, a quest for an antigravity propulsion system was conducted by the USAF Science Applications International Corporation on behalf of USAF's then Astronautics Laboratory at Edwards AFB. (Area 51 is a detachment of Edwards ABF, which is responsible for testing of advanced flying vehicles). British multinational defence and aerospace company BAE Systems also provided internal resources for its own antigravity studies.

However, there was no significant progress in this area. At least not officially.

In the late 1990's, Dr. Musha says he worked with the Honda Corporation Research Institute in Japan and conducted an experiment to confirm the electrogravitic effect.

Astonishingly, Dr. Musha claims he and the Honda Corporation obtained a positive result.

Dr. Musha also says, "In Dr. Thomas Valone's 1993 book *Electrogravitics Systems: Reports on a New Propulsion Methodology,* Dr. Paul LaViolette claimed that electrogravitic technology was developed under US Air Force black projects since late 1954, and it may now have been put to practical use in the B-2 Advanced Technology Bomber to provide an exotic auxiliary mode of propulsion."

Dr. Musha continues, "An electrogravitic drive of B-2 could allow it to fly at a sufficiently high speed at high altitude, or even (in) space, and it could fly around the world without refueling in an antigravity mode."

In his paper *Connection Between Einstein's Unified Field Theory and the Biefeld-Brown Effect,* Dr. Musha mentioned a follow-up experiment to his one with the Honda Corporation in the 1990's. It was conducted at Meisei University in Tokyo in 2003. According to Dr. Musha, the experiment involved "manufacturing a giant lifter." The scientists at the university succeeded in raising the lifter into the air where it hovered with complete stability at 15 meters (approximately 50 feet) above the ground inside the university's gymnasium.

Experiments involving lifters (also known as ionocrafts or ion-propelled crafts), which

Above: A giant lifter hovers in the air during a 2003 experiment at Meisei University

produce thrust in the air without any moving parts or combustion, are quite controversial in academic circles. Some scientists believe these craft are propelled solely by ion winds while others say they involve at least some antigravitational forces.

"Lifters are basically very primitive antigravity devices," says Dr. Musha. "Most scientists believe they are propelled by the ion wind generated by high potential electric fields, but it is not true. The Meisei University experiment appears to prove this. Some of the force that lifted the craft in that experiment was antigravitational because it was very stable as it hovered in the air inside the room. Ion wind cannot hover a giant craft in a stable fashion inside a room as shown in the photo."

All this confirms once again that science, and especially suppressed or classified science, may have long-ago evolved to the point where building antigravity spacecraft has been entirely possible.

Possible, that is, *without any assistance from ET civilizations.*

9

• • • ● ● ● ● ● • • •

REVERSE ENGINEERING

There's a third scenario in the human versus alien debate regarding antigravity technologies.

This scenario would see a combination of the two extremes—meaning it isn't fully human technology and isn't fully alien, but a hybrid, or fusion, of the two.

The theory suggests alien technology somehow arrived on Earth in the mid-20th Century in an event like the 1947 Roswell crash. A flying saucer was found and then reverse-engineered by reproducing the alien inventor's product after careful study.

The aforementioned claims of Area 51 employee Bob Lazar would fit into this category. Besides Lazar, many other ex-military personnel have claimed the US did indeed successfully reverse-engineer recovered ET spacecraft and eventually learn how to manufacture such antigravity craft en masse.

"Many of the engineers I interviewed worked on reverse-engineering technology. It's a hallmark of Area 51."

–Annie Jacobsen, from a Democracy Now TV interview discussing her book Area 51: An Uncensored History of America's Top Secret Military Base.

Reverse engineering, incidentally, is the reproduction of another manufacturer's product following detailed examination of its construction or composition.

After the Roswell crash, there were reports in the following months and years of successive UFO crashes in America. Which raises the question: Were technologies gained by the US via reverse engineering recovered craft from these crash sites?

According to Colonel Philip J. Corso's writings in his aforementioned book *The Day After Roswell,* the UFO craft recovered at Roswell seemed to have the ability to store as

Above: Fiber optics—extraterrestrial technology?

*"LED Glasfaser" by Oliver Deisenroth—Own work.
Licensed under GFDL via Wikimedia Commons*

well as conduct a vast amount of electric current. He suspected the craft was simply a capacitor that stored current controlled or vectored by the pilot and able to recharge itself with some form of built-in generator, just like a very advanced flying battery.

Corso believed if this craft was propelled by electromagnetic antigravity propulsion, its flight might be greatly influenced by outer electric fields. Hence its flight could be disturbed by a thunder storm or radiation of strong electromagnetic fields such as radar systems.

From the debris of crashed UFO's, so Corso claims, US scientists invented integrated circuit chips, fiber optics, lasers and super-tenacity fibers by using the reverse engineering techniques.

If these theories are true, then besides classified exotic inventions like flying saucers, most modern technologies available to the public, such as computers and smart phones, may in fact be extraterrestrial in origin.

"I have contact with certain diplomats who not only confirm meetings have been taking place between some government officials and an alien race, but have been receiving assistance from this race to advance technology to enable us to meet hostile aliens on a level

playing field. My contacts have been present at these meetings and have met these aliens who are benevolent towards us but will not act with aggression towards any life form unless in self defence, but they are prepared to help us advance our technology."

–Tony Dodd. Former British police officer.

10

· · · ● ● ● ● ● ● · · ·

Other UFO Theories

Could there be other theories, not covered (so far) in this book, that more aptly match the actual reality of the UFO phenomenon? Even something besides the obvious possibilities of human *or* alien, or human *and* alien, technologies?

Furthermore, could the truth be something stranger, or more malicious, or even more *out there* than anything most researchers would ever stop to consider let alone write about?

In a 2014 interview with host Sean Stone on the alternative views talk show *Buzzsaw,* one of the world's leading UFO investigators, Richard Dolan, told how Jimmy Carter reacted when informed of the truth about UFO's upon becoming US President.

Dolan said, "This is a story that I was told, but again I credit this source, of when Jimmy Carter, wanted to get a briefing. Now Jimmy Carter becomes President in January 1977, a long time ago now. He had talked as a candidate about having seen a UFO.

"Jimmy Carter comes into the White House in 1977 and he seems to have gotten a briefing on this subject in June of that year. Now according to the gentleman I had a detailed conversation with about this, and it was not known to this gentleman what was said to Carter, but it was known to him that at the end of the briefing Carter was deeply upset . . . And that he was seen literally at his desk, elbows on the desk, head in his hands, and apparently sobbing."

So the question that must be asked would be what sort of truths about UFO's would make an intelligent, worldly President break down and cry in that fashion? And whatever those truths are, does their shocking nature explain why they are being withheld from the public?

In the same interview, Dolan also brought up a fascinating idea that had occurred to him after decades of researching UFO reports all over the world: that we may be looking at things all wrong by blaming governments and their

Above: President Carter shocked by the truth about UFO's

*"JimmyCarterPortrait" by Department of Defense
Department of the Navy. Naval Photographic Center
Licensed under Public Domain via Wikimedia Commons*

Above: Lockheed Martin calling the shots?

*"LockheedMartinLogo" by Lockheed Martin
Licensed under Public Domain via Wikimedia Commons*

intelligence agencies for covering up antigravity technologies.

"The way I think these things work," Dolan told Sean Stone, "is that the secret becomes privatized increasingly. And again I would emphasize for people to look at the general structure of the US military and to see how that has become privatized. And how secrecy itself has become privatized.

"In other words," Dolan continued, "if we were working in a black budget program, what are called special access programs, and let's say I was a Defense Department person and you were a person at Lockheed Martin . . . You'd be the contractor and chances are you would have more power in the program than I would. The private contractors, as far as we can determine on these black budget programs, have the upper hand and they really run the show. The secret in other words is not so much classified as it is proprietary . . . And that appears to me to be how the UFO secret has gone."

And finally, what if UFO's are not physical objects like planes or space rockets, but are instead some kind of quantum physics-esque, interdimensional or multidimensional, time traveling, teleporting objects?

The *interdimensional hypothesis,* which is completely different to the *extraterrestrial hypothesis,* has been written about by

Ufologists such as Jacques Vallée and others. It basically suggests that UFO sightings and interrelated events such as alien abductions, crop circles and cattle mutilations, all involve *visitations* from other dimensions, or planes of existence, or parallel worlds, that exist simultaneously to our reality.

While this idea may sound ridiculous, it probably cannot be easily dismissed as there have been numerous declassified documents that seem to indicate the militaries of the world have no idea what UFO's actually are.

If the interdimensional theory is true, then perhaps antigravity flying machines have the ability to bend space and time via black holes, worm holes or whatever. And maybe they also have the ability to just appear in our world from out of nowhere . . .

Above: Anomaly captured on a digital camera

*"062102mj842pm" by Mahtomj—Own work
Licensed under CC BY-SA 3.0 via Wikimedia Commons*

CONNECTING THE DOTS

· · · • • ● ● ● • • · ·

"The reality is that they (aliens) have been visiting earth for decades and probably millennia and have contributed considerably to our knowledge."

–Paul Hellyer (Canada's former Minister of National Defence) from an interview with the Canadian Press in 2010.

So what is the truth regarding the antigravity spacecraft that Area 51 appears to be concealing? Are such technologies manmade or alien, or a combination of the two?

In short, after researching this subject for quite some time, we still have no idea!

However, if you really want our guess, and it most certainly would be a guess, we think there are enough eyewitness accounts and testimonials from former military and intelligence personnel to suggest aliens not only exist, but have already visited Planet Earth. And it's our guess the highest levels of the world's governments are aware of this.

Therefore, we believe that antigravity propulsion systems seen by UFO witnesses are most likely human/alien (hybrid) technologies that have been reverse engineered after alien craft were recovered at crash sites.

Perhaps it would be wise to defer to former Canadian Defence Minister Paul Hellyer, the man nicknamed *the highest-ranked alien believer on Earth,* who has said on the record that extraterrestrials are already living among us, but refuse to share their most advanced technology because of humanity's refusal to stop wars.

The now retired politician and engineer claims to have directly witnessed UFO technology and confirmed the existence of alien beings on Earth through his high-level political and military contacts in Canada and the United States.

On January 1, 2014, Hellyer told news outlet *Russia Today* he believes there are about 80

Above: Ex-Canadian politician Paul Hellyer—alien believer

"Paul Hellyer-c1969" by Themightyquill—Own work
Licensed under CC BY-SA 3.0 via Wikimedia Commons

different species of ETs, some of whom "look just like us and they could walk down the street and you wouldn't know if you walked past one . . . I would say that nearly all are benign and benevolent and they do want to help us, there may be one or two species which do not."

Hellyer also told *Russia Today* that aliens are not that impressed by humans. "They don't think we are good stewards of our planet, we're clear cutting our forests, we're polluting our rivers and our lakes, and we're dumping sewage in the oceans, and we're doing all sorts of things which are not what good stewards of their homes should be doing."

Canada's former Defence Minister has repeatedly begged governments around the world to disclose ET technology for the benefit of Mankind, in particular technology that could resolve the problem of climate change.

For example, on February 28, 2007, he told the *Ottawa Citizen:* "I would like to see what (alien) technology there might be that could eliminate the burning of fossil fuels within a generation . . . that could be a way to save our planet . . . We need to persuade governments to come clean on what they know. Some of us suspect they know quite a lot, and it might be enough to save our planet if applied quickly enough."

If Hellyer is correct in what he says, this further confirms the existence of the Splinter Civilization we have theorized on and speculated about throughout this book. His comments also support our contention that nothing's more important for the planet right now than releasing all the scientific breakthroughs and technologies that are currently being suppressed or otherwise classified by the Splinter Civilization.

Whether these technologies are of alien origin (*a la* Roswell) or are of the human variety (*a la* Tesla), we firmly believe they could not only solve climate change, as Hellyer suggests, but also solve an infinite number of other critical problems that currently plague the planet.

The danger is if the collective thinking of the public at large remains closed to the possibility of such technologies existing, the likelihood of these problems being solved any time soon looks remote.

A major mind-shift is required. That doesn't mean buying into every conspiracy theory out there, but it does mean keeping—or adopting, whichever the case—an open mind so that all possibilities can be considered.

Perhaps that mind-shift may be similar to what US astronomer Carl Sagan was referring to when he said in a speech he gave in Seattle,

Washington in June, 1994, "The truth may be puzzling. It may take some work to grapple with. It may be counterintuitive. It may contradict deeply held prejudices. It may not be consonant with what we desperately want to be true. But our preferences do not determine what's true."

We also happen to believe all truths are eventually revealed in time. No secrets can be kept buried forever.

It's a bit like how the origins of early Christianity are now acknowledged by most historians and theologians to differ in many ways from the official account. One example in this analogy is how the extensive Fourth Century Biblical edits made by the Romans are all now fairly common knowledge, at least in academic and theology circles. Well, probably the same thing will happen in time with Roswell and the entire alien cover-up—or alien myth, depending on your take.

One way or another, humanity as a whole will one day know for sure whether the antigravity flying discs so many are seeing in the skies are manmade or alien tech. Likewise, the history of the elite levels of certain governments interacting with extraterrestrial civilizations will also surface, if indeed it is true.

As William Shakespeare wrote all those centuries ago, "The truth will out."

AFTERWORD

• • • ● ● ● ● ● • • •

This well balanced and unbiased book is long overdue for those searching for the truth about advanced technologies currently being concealed from the general populace by elite levels of governments.

Formerly, I was employed for many years as a senior research scientist developing naval underwater weapon systems at the Technical Research and Development Institute of the Ministry of Defense in Japan.

I was also part of a team of scientists in the Advanced Space Propulsion Investigation Committee (ASPIC), which was organized by the Japan Society for Aeronautical and Space Sciences in 1994. ASPIC's purpose was to study all kinds of non-chemical space propulsion systems as opposed to conventional rocket systems for space missions to nearby planets, the Moon and the outer Solar System. This included field propulsion systems which utilize zero-point energy, the electrogravitic effect and the non-Newtonian gravitic effect predicted in Einstein's Theory of Gravity.

During my time with ASPIC, I strongly felt that some of the gravity control systems could have been realized, or had already been realized, but were being overshadowed by existing science.

Spiraling out of my activities as a member of ASPIC, I wrote a book in collaboration with Professor Mário Pinheiro, of Portugal, and Dr. Thomas Valone, of the Integrity Research Institute, in the US, titled *Gravitoelectromagnetic Theories and Their Applications to Advanced Science and Technology* (published by Nova Science Publishers, in New York). That book describes how gravitoelectromagnetism refers to a set of formal correlations between the equations for relativistic gravitation and electromagnetism.

The book also mentions how T.T. Brown, who initially discovered the electrogravitic effect, performed several experiments during the 1950's and succeeded in generating thrust without the reliance on a surrounding medium by applying high voltage to materials with high dielectric constants.

Thomas Valone's 1993 book, *Electrogravitics Systems: Reports on a New Propulsion Methodology,* quotes antigravity researcher Dr. Paul LaViolette as saying electrogravitic technology was first developed under a US Air Force black project in 1954. Valone's book also alleges that the top-secret technology has since been used in the B-2 stealth bomber to provide an exotic auxiliary mode of propulsion.

Once I had a chance to read Colonel Philip J. Corso's *The Day After Roswell,* which rates a mention in this book, I was astonished to learn the Roswell crashed UFO was, according to the colonel, propelled by a technology that sounded remarkably similar to the electrogravitic system developed by the US Air Force.

What could be behind this apparent coincidence? In *Antigravity Propulsion,* James & Lance Morcan have pointed out the possible connection between the Nazis, Japan and the Roswell UFO crash.

There have been little-known but persistent rumors that the Nazis obtained advanced technologies from extraterrestrial entities or descendants of a highly advanced civilization that existed in prehistoric times. Before and during World War Two, there were said to be exchanges of information between the Nazis and the Japanese Government relating to exotic sciences and technologies from other (ancient) civilizations.

Also during this same period, it is known that the Nazis spent a large amount of time, resources and manpower on their mission to discover the origins of the Aryan race. They made several expeditions to Tibet and came to the conclusion that Tibetans were ancestors of the Aryans. The Nazis therefore considered it acceptable to view the Tibetans as an intermediary race between the Germans and the Japanese.

Perhaps in the Tibetan culture the Nazis also uncovered advanced knowledge which allowed them to develop their highly evolved sciences.

I was once informed by a military contact who worked for a period at an Air Force base that the *beings* of crashed UFO's had a human-like stature similar to Asian people (especially Japanese), but when anatomical dissections were made they were found to have a highly developed endocrine system not previously seen before.

Thus, I suppose, there is a possibility that what we call *aliens* are actually human beings evolved from the common ancestors of our human race. *They* might have been the ones the Nazis wanted to contact during their Tibetan expeditions and may have also been a crucial

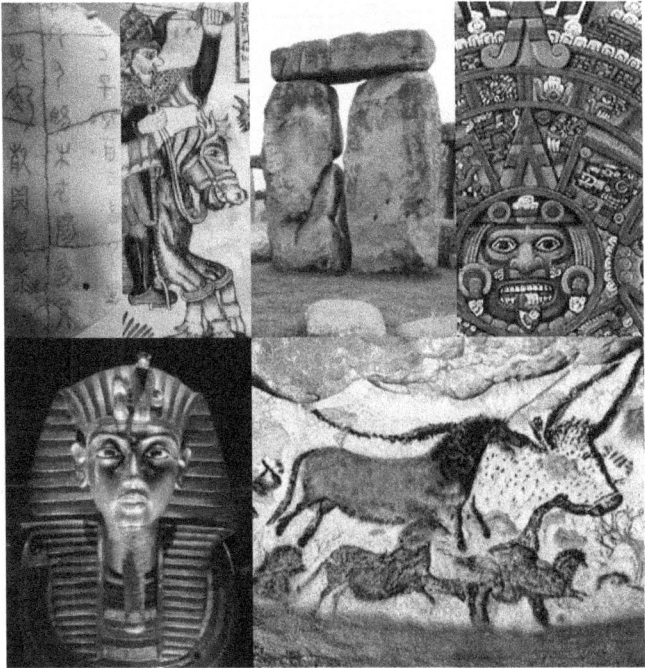

Above: Ancient civilizations might be more advanced scientifically than academia supposes?

*"Wikijunior Ancient Civilizations Composite" by William R. Wilson—Original Composite
Licensed under CC BY-SA 3.0 via Wikimedia Commons*

Above: A fake (or real?) image of some kind of construction
on the Moon

component in the Third Reich's bid to gain superior technologies.

Probably, these ancient human/alien beings are still working in Earth's neighborhood as well as in our Solar System, using their advanced technologies. Hence, I suspect, the main purpose of suppressing certain aspects of the Apollo Moon missions and NASA's other explorations was to investigate these *other* beings' activities in Outer Space.

After the Roswell crash, it is possible some of these ancient beings' advanced technologies were transferred to US military forces as per the reverse engineering theory the Morcans cover in this book.

However, for the time being at least, the origins of these technologies still remain a mystery waiting to be solved.

Dr. Takaaki Musha

Director of the Advanced-Science Technology Research Organization, Yokohama, Japan.

Former senior research scientist at the Technical Research and Development Institute of the Ministry of Defense, Japan.

THE END

If you liked this book, the authors would greatly appreciate a review from you on Amazon.

OTHER BOOKS

· · · ● ● ● ● ● · · ·

BY JAMES & LANCE MORCAN PUBLISHED BY
STERLING GATE BOOKS

NON-FICTION:

DEBUNKING HOLOCAUST DENIAL THEORIES: Two
Non-Jews Affirm the Historicity of the Nazi
Genocide

THE ORPHAN CONSPIRACIES: 29 Conspiracy
Theories from The Orphan Trilogy

GENIUS INTELLIGENCE: Secret Techniques and
Technologies to Increase IQ (The Underground
Knowledge Series, #1)

HISTORICAL FICTION:

Into the Americas (A novel based on a true story)

World Odyssey (The World Duology, #1)

Fiji: A Novel (The World Duology, #2)

White Spirit (A novel based on a true story)

THRILLERS:

The Ninth Orphan (The Orphan Trilogy, #1)

The Orphan Factory (The Orphan Trilogy, #2)

The Orphan Uprising (The Orphan Trilogy, #3)

www.ingramcontent.com/pod-product-compliance
Lightning Source LLC
LaVergne TN
LVHW011334080426
835513LV00006B/340